*For my children, Craig and Sarah who are my real achievement in life*

*And my granddaughter Emily. My reason to breathe.*

*"Children are repository of infinite possibilities".*

*Andrew Jackson Davies*

# CONTENTS.

# Forward.

Since I began to teach mediumship it has amazed me how easily influenced students are. In their rush to become 'professionals' they hang on to every-word their 'teacher' tells them I am constantly asking my students to become their own scientists, to use their logical minds in their quest to advance their discipline, and not to just believe what I am saying to them. After all I am only human, a mere mortal, I am not always right. Then one day I was telling students how my development days were and I realised that I too was that gullible once over, and I hung on to my teacher's every word

So this book is for two reasons. First it is to highlight just how naive we become when we seek out this power we call mediumship and secondly to offer some guidance for the student on their development. I hope that by taking the reader on a journey through my own development, and showing the heartache and humorous times I personally had you will realise the importance of keeping a reasoning mind, But also to give some practical advice for your own journey.

I often say that the Spirit world do not want sheep, but they do want critical thinkers who will question what is happening to them on their road of growth and discovery.

I hope you will enjoy the reading of this little book, but more importantly I hope it shows you how far we have progressed in the teaching and understanding of mediumship, that this will help you to go forward in your own development with an open and clear mind.

## Chapter 1.

## The Beginning.

"Where do you think mam is?" So began a conversation that would change my life forever.

My mother had died when I was sixteen, she had a long illness with depression. Mum had been brought up in a large Catholic family and had been married twice. Her first marriage the love of her life was a Scottish man called Bill who was 10 years older than her and a non- Catholic. Her own mother had died at an early age which left her to raise her siblings and take care of her father. Mam had made two errors in her young life the first was she married a non- catholic and also he had been married before, these were big sins in the eyes of the church and in my opinion added to her guilt and subsequent mental illness. She had in total six children; 3 sons a gap then myself and my younger brother and sister.

 Mam had made my young life hell because of her mental health problems to say I came from a dysfunctional family is an understatement I do not remember a time when the house was ever empty or happy. The family consisted of Mam, her father my granddad (a devout catholic and bigot who could always recite his rosaries no matter how drunk he was) my mum's brother who was disabled, my younger sister and Brother, also for a short time my step father and his two daughters. Life was very difficult with mams illness and she spent many days in bed unable to cope with the pressures of life, after her death, which was in the March I got married in the July with hindsight probably to fulfil my yearning to be part of a family, I was already pregnant with my eldest daughter, when I was 17 she was born and two years later my second daughter came along, six years later my son.

Looking after my family and the responsibility of my brother and sister was quite a lot to cope with but as there were no other options I didn't really think about it.

It was 10 years later whilst cooking tea for my younger sister who was just thirteen when mam passed away, she asked me the question; "where do you think mam is"? To which I replied, without hesitation Hell. I had been brought up in a Catholic family so it seemed the only possible answer after all is this not where all bad people go?

But my sister did not give up asking me "should we go to the spook church to find out"? (For those not familiar with this expression it is a slang name for a Spiritualist Church that we use in the North of England). Well to be honest I nearly fainted, "no absolutely not", images of hell and burning flames filled my mind at the thought. What on earth was my Sister thinking about asking such a question? I was so influenced by my Grandfathers Catholic outlook, as a child I had attended bible class and was expected to become a nun eventually, my grandfather often said there was a wanting in me that had to be knocked out, and he believed the church could do this. I still don't know what he meant by this expression.

"There's a service on Thursday at 'Boro' road we could go and see, it won't hurt" prompted my sister.

For those of you who are not familiar with Spiritualism, it has been a legal religion since 1951 and as holds services within their churches. A service consists usually of prayer, hymns and a philosophy about the religion's beliefs based on the seven principles followed by a demonstration of mediumship.

Eventually after much persuading I agreed to go with my sister to church, to be honest my sister could usually talk me into anything she was the youngest of six children, she tended to get her own way a lot I also had three older brothers who were all living their own lives with their own families.

So it was agreed, on Thursday at 6.45 I was to meet my sister at the doors of this church, when the time came my husband drove me to the church and I waited for my sister. "Go in then" my husband said "I am not sitting here all night", reluctantly I left the safety of the car and stood outside the church doors I remember trembling with fear and the sick feeling in the pit of my stomach all the teaching and indoctrination I had from the Catholic church had really filled me with dread. I watched as lots of people were going into this church which was only an end street house in a not very nice part of town it faced a very busy road and is opposite a public house and it has been known for drunks to wander into the church, mistaking it for the pub across the street.

Middlesbrough is an industrial town in the North East of England. It once thrived with industries like ICI and British Steel but over the years these industries have declined and the town has struggled to survive, like most towns we have drug problems and the part of town the church is in has a lot of areas were drugs were available. I stood there not really knowing what I was most afraid of going into church or getting robbed, I checked my watch again and again still no sister, then a pleasant looking lady stood at the door way and asked me to come in, 'no I am waiting for someone' I replied, they may be already in, why don't you come in and have a look. She smiled again at me.

Well against my better judgement I did trembling I walked through the door half expecting a human sacrifice on the altar and most definitely expecting it to be illuminated with candles, but it was nothing like that at all, sparsely decorated with wooden seats and full to the brim with people all ages, all sizes. To my horror there was only one seat left, right at the front as I sat down I glanced up to the altar in front of me, (which I now know is called a rostrum, a platform or stage which the speakers stand upon.) There standing looking back at everyone, was a lady who was the speaker for the evening, and a gentleman who was the chairman. The gentleman stood up first and introduced the medium for the evening, a very smart well-spoken gentleman who told the audience what to expect and a little information about the medium, the medium then took over the service she first did a prayer followed by a hymn and then a philosophy about how she came into Spiritualism, we sang a couple of hymns and I started to relax a little after all I was comfortable with prayer and hymns and to my surprise the prayer was to God not the Devil as I had expected, and her talk was quite interesting.

I kept looking behind me nervously still no sign of my sister, then to my horror the medium asked could she speak to me! I looked at other people sitting next to me surely she means them? I half hoped half prayed but she didn't wait for

6

me to answer her. "I have your father here he was very ill when he died and you were very young he loves you very much". (My dad died when I was 6 he had pancreatic cancer). I began to cry and then sob it was as though the pain of losing both parents was finally released in one go and I couldn't stop crying almost wailing I was aware of people looking at me, then the lady who had first invited me in offered me a tissue. That was until the medium said, "one day you will stand here" and pointed to the rostrum, the tears stopped I looked her right in the eye "you're mad" I said and walked out.

My sister didn't come to the church she informed me the next day she had forgotten all about it, I told her about my message which she thought was amazing but because she had even less recollection of dad than me she was more confused why mam wasn't with him.

The message troubled my mind every day I couldn't sleep thinking about it, how did the medium know about my dad who could have told her? What does God think about this, I contemplated speaking to the priest but somehow it didn't seem right either?

What I did know was that I would not go back.

But eventually I did go back to the small Spiritualist church and listened to other speakers but I never got another message. The church although full were mainly full of older people, people who had grown up with Spiritualism. Like a lovely lady called Ruby her whole family had been Spiritualists and had witnessed many forms of mediumship including physical mediumship.

I was still torn between the buzz of going back and the disloyalty to God and my church I thought that God would be very unhappy with me going into this place, it is funny how a strong religious influence can dominate your life.

I told my older brother about what had happened and the message off dad from the medium, he told me that my dad's mam Jessie had been a medium in Motherwell near to Glasgow and she had died long before I was born no one had told me anything about my Dads side of the family, I wondered if my father had any experiences of these churches but my brother didn't know. It was information that I didn't really connect to until much later in my life.

7

One evening while sitting in Boro road church I heard some people talking about another church in town that had a development group so I asked them what that was? They explained to me it was where you go to develop mediumship, I was intrigued so you could actually learn to do this? I had never even thought that there could be classes to teach you this. I never knew that mediums could be taught; I thought they were somehow special and had these gifts all their lives. So the following Saturday I went along to this church. It was I learned, a Christian Spiritualist Church there are two different types a Christian Spiritualist accepts the leadership of Jesus Christ and they follow the bible teachings and the Spiritualist National Union which follows the seven principles and one of them is personal responsibility and does not believe anyone can die for our 'sins'.

The Christian church was again in the centre of town, and once again a converted end terraced house, inside it was a lot more nicely decorated and had familiar pictures on Jesus on the walls crosses and even a Bible on the lectern, I have to admit because of the familiar artefacts I felt a lot more at home here. Saturday night was open circle night; this is where trainee mediums could practice giving messages, People would sit in a large circle and would open with a prayer and sing a hymn, it was a lot more relaxed on these nights with no philosophy and as many people who want to give messages can do so. I approached a very friendly smiling lady who was selling the raffle tickets, (I found this very odd, raffle tickets on sale in a church you could win a packet of biscuits or a bottle of bubble bath in a church!) I asked about joining the development group, "Oh you have to speak to the lady who runs it she won't be in till tomorrow night our Divine service". The next night I went along again, and I have to admit I enjoyed the comfortable surroundings and the friendliness of the people they certainly were more open than in the church I was used to people said hello and smiled. Again the church was mainly made up of older people and again they saw the church as their religion and accepted it very naturally.

The lady I had spoken to the night before was there again, 'that is who you need to speak to she whispered' and pointed to a lady opposite, on the other side of the church was a lady probably in her sixties greying hair and nicely rounded it seemed everyone knew her and clamoured to speak to her, She reminded me of the queen mother with an entourage around her; she certainly got a lot of respect. So I took a deep breath and walked over "can I join your group please" she looked me up and down and said, "Come along on Wednesday meet the rest of the group if they approve you can join".

As easy as that I couldn't believe it no questions I didn't have to give a reason and the speech I had prepared in my mind just in case was not needed. I went home and informed my husband and children and as I expected none of them were really bothered that I was going to this funny church my husband and I were not the best at communicating anyway so if he was happy or unhappy about it he never said, my children just said "if you want to go, then go". I went along the following Wednesday with a mixture of feeling intrigued, scared and excited.

This is the beginning of my journey into mediumship. A journey that would transform my life in a way that no one least of all me, would ever imagine.

# Chapter 2.

## *THE GROUP.*

Wednesday came around quickly and I turned up at the church early not wanting to be late on my first night. There were already a group of people standing in the street smoking and chatting so I timidly went to join them, one lady caught my eye and as I searched my brain trying to remember where I knew her from it suddenly clicked, "is your name Maureen" I asked "who wants to know" she replied, my name was Jackie Bell my mam was Betty her and your mam were friends, her face softened and she said "yes that's right I remember". Maureen is a 'what you see is what you get' kind of lady and she was my closest ally on my journey into church and development. Maureen has become a firm friend and to this day she has supported me through more heartache than any other living person and I care about her very much.

The group was large we were about 14 in total and very mixed mainly women and one guy. All different ages and walks of life and all had their own problems and heartache to tell but also they all knew each other very well so I was the new kid at school. I met lots of people like an elderly lady who read the tarot and the tea leaves, the lady who I met on my first visit to the church a younger lady who ran a judo group her name was little Mo although to be honest she frightened the life out of me, she certainly had issues with rage, a lady who was very experienced and was the teacher's helper and stand in at times, Maureen of course, myself and a few other that came and went. Although we were from different backgrounds, what we had in common was that we were all broken in some way we all had a story to tell, one lady who came along with her sister had a lost her son to suicide, a Lady who worked a lot with crystals we call to this day crystal Sue, Kath very much the 'mother' of the group who son had died tragically in a car crash, it became very evident we all needed, and got something from the church not necessarily to do with development in mediumship.

When we got into the church it was the same room I had been in for the Divine service but now the chairs were set out in a circle, there was soft music playing and it was well lit for some reason this was important to me that there was plenty of light. everybody initially headed upstairs, in its original use,

 this would have been the bedrooms but now one room was transformed into a kitchen that was for the teacher and privileged few to enter only, then a toilet, a second room which was more of a store room and the third room was full of chairs were we sat for tea and coffee. In a way I loved this social side more than the training when we all got together in the upstairs room I felt I belonged here, there was a buzz and an expectation almost as we sat together mostly we listened to each member talking about the great things that had happened to them that week and how Spirit had woken them from their sleep to give fabulous information. I never once thought is it true? I sat wide eyed listening to each incredible story, occasionally Maureen would nudge me and raise her eyebrows in disbelief but I soaked it all in, then we would be called to go down stairs, 7pm on the dot Spirit would not wait for us and we should never be late.

We started with an introduction, I had to tell the group my name and where I lived and they in turn did the same, I was a little scared after all if the group didn't accept me I was out. The entire group told me their names and then a meditation started. This was where I first struggled I had never meditated in my life what was it? How did you do it? I listened to our teacher take us on a wonderful journey into the woods and listening to the birds in the trees then across a lake, wonderful but I couldn't keep up; there were long gaps in my mind where I just lost the thread and my mind kept reminding me that I didn't have enough milk for the breakfasts in the morning, no one had asked me if I had done one before or explained the process, I didn't know what I should experience. Afterwards the teacher told us to come back which really was not difficult because I had not gone anywhere to come back from, she asked us all what we got, "well there were beautiful colours" said one, "I met my dad" said another," I met a native American Indian" said another. As she went round each person their journeys got more elaborate than the last Oh God I thought, what will I say? "So Jackie what did you get"? "Not a lot really I lost your voice a little" I replied nervously, that was the first time I encountered the teachers disapproving look, with a slight shake of her head she said almost under her breath "oh you will need a lot of work". And carried on to the next person who had seen lots of crystals and an old man who asked her to take the crystals, I felt so inadequate why couldn't I see all of this? The teacher then went on to ask us to open up, she told us to close our eyes and visualise a closed flower at the base chakra and to see it slowly climbing to the sacral chakra then the solar plexus and at each chakra the flower would open a little more all the way to the heart the throat the third eye and finally the crown. "It is important that you open these chakras properly or you will not be able to work" said this wise teacher she had so much knowledge that I didn't dare tell her that I couldn't for the life of me see a flower open or shut, oh God I was doomed I had no clue what a chakra was, in fact it was some months later while reading a book that I first knew that anything about chakras, I kept thinking if I have these in my body why haven't I heard about them before are they part of my organs? (I now know, chakras are invisible energy centres very much an eastern belief system and I also now know they don't have anything what so ever to do with mediumship or its development).

Then came our next piece of valuable advice, "Remember to put on your cloak of protection you should NEVER begin working until you have on your cloak of protection". (I fully understand if the reader now has a vision of Harry Potter in their mind). I could wait no longer my knees were trembling as I shakily raised my hand, the teacher looked towards me over the rim of her spectacles, "could you tell me why and what is protection" I asked; she half raised her eyebrows slowly looked around the group "to keep you safe from low and evil Spirits of course, do you think it is all love and light in the Spirit world". I was dumbstruck I had never even considered that we could be visited by evil Spirits, who was I kidding in truth I had never even considered been visited by any kind of Spirit.

The evening continued with various discussions, the group had homework from the week before so the teacher listened to all their thoughts and told them where they went wrong, in honesty most of them were wrong but they never got a full explanation as to why, At the end of the evening a member of the group was elected to close in prayer and we had to 'shut down' the opposite way to how we opened up ensuring that the flower was tightly closed before we left the circle, once again I saw nothing. Very soon the night was over we all went back upstairs to the little tea room and chatted about different things, some of the group did private sittings other were preparing for an up- coming fledgling night (this is where trainee mediums take part in a service giving messages, philosophy and prayer under the watchful eye of an experienced medium.) I sat close to my new friend Maureen who I came to rely on a lot and I asked her about the opening up and closing down procedure, "do you do that every time" I asked. "of course if we don't we can get all kinds of evil Spirits attaching themselves to us so I close down with the flower I then shut doors over them, and of course I lock the doors and then I get a security guard to stand at the doors to make sure no one gets in". I stared at her in disbelief was it really that dangerous could I really be possessed by evil Spirits? On my journey home and in bed that night I thought about this, what on earth I was doing getting involved in something so dangerous. In my mind I could hear my mam telling me how stupid I was to be doing this sort of thing and it would be me that would go to hell. (This was not unusual with my mam when she was alive she often told me I was stupid, inadequate and that the devil was waiting for me, the 'voice' I could hear of course was the memoires she left me with not her actual Spirit voice).

This troubled me all week, but when Wednesday came again and I found myself getting ready to go back. My head was telling me not to but there was a feeling that I couldn't explain that pulled me back. To be on the safe side I said a long and dutiful prayer to God and asked him to protect my soul while I was there. The night started very much as the last prayer, opening up, protection and meditation. I noticed that certain people were very much favoured by the teacher and certainly considered to be 'good students', I also noticed the competition that existed to be noticed by the teacher and receive her praise, but I could not understand why nobody ever asked a question or why they were doing certain exercises, they just accepted that when they were told to do something it was right to do.

Now at this point I must explain something to you readers, you see I never really had an academic education because of mam's illness I never really had that much schooling, practically none existent when I came to secondary school. I tell you this because I never considered myself very bright so the fact that I was not getting the instructions correctly was surely down to me being thick after all everyone else was understanding, weren't they?

The weeks turned into months and I began to notice that people within the group had all been through some kind of trauma, bad childhood's bad marriages bereavement and in truth with hindsight, it was probably more of a counselling self-help group than a serious structured development group. But for me the sheer frustration at not knowing what I was meant to be doing and not understanding the terminology that the teacher used was starting to get me down, I really began to question why I was giving up this time plus my husband was letting me know he was not happy about the time I was spending at this church and with this group. One evening, frustrated by my lack of progress or knowledge I started to ask questions like why or how, I could hear the groans from the group as I put my hand up again, and the roll of the teacher's eyes when I asked a question. Very rarely did I get a reply, I was invariably told to just get on with the exercise and it would become clear with practice but it never ever did.

One week the teacher told us she would teach us all about healing. Healing she said was a very important part of Spirit's work and we all needed to learn how to be clear channels for the healing energy. I was slightly excited about this I suppose in truth I was hoping it would be something I could do as I seemed to be failing at everything else. So it began a student had to pretend to be the patient, we the healers had to attune to the Spirit world which meant we had to ensure we had our protection in place and had opened up our chakras, a short meditation took place, and we were ready to begin. "Jackie stand behind your patient" I did so straight away, 'now begin healing' my heart sank I looked towards the teacher, "erm how"? the famous roll of the eyes began and she sighed heavily. To this day I get un-nerved by a person sighing at me or rolling their eyes probably because of my childhood, it reminds me how inadequate I am and my teacher reminded me of this point every single week.  "Put your hand on her shoulders then feel the energy field" I did so but truthfully I could no more feel the energy field than see the man on the moon, "now move your hands down over the body, slowly" she barked, I did as I was told until I was laying on the floor with my hands on the student/ patients feet then made my way on all fours around to the front of the patient and began working my way up the body.

"Ok" said the teacher to the patient "what did you feel"? "Oh I saw lots of colours and felt heat" said the dutiful patient. Oh thank the Lord; I thought I wanted to shout out halleluiah she could see colours because of my healing, I could do something after all.

This euphoria was short lived we soon went back to the giving messages but I found it so frustrating sitting there waiting for the Spirit world to drop by and the slim chance I would catch them as they did. I had some hits, I would often pick up on another student's problem in life which was met with a huge roar of approval but with hindsight my messages lacked depth. We did all kinds of exercises, one was the flower reading exercise we would be instructed to pick a flower on route to class on no account must we buy one or allow someone else to touch it. I looked long and hard for the right flower but not being much of a gardener I ended up borrowing one from someone's garden on route to church. Once in class we all had to put the flowers on a tray while another student gave us a reading without knowing whose flower was whose. 'This person has had a difficult life' so began one reading, "the stem has thorns so there has been people attacking them but the flower itself is strong so they will survive." I was mesmerised how could this information be got from a random flower? so true to form I raised my hand, "please could you tell me how this works, how did the student get that information", the teacher looked me straight in the eye and said "by linking into the energy of the flower it told the student the information", I was even more confused how could a flower know this about the student? But I knew better than to carry on asking (Of course I now know the flower is a tool the medium actually links to the energy of the person they are reading for).

My teacher worked full time in a very responsible job there were times she could not attend when this happened we were tutored by a more experienced student who had been in this group for years and already did private sittings professionally. This lady had a kindly disposition and was also well rounded, I once asked why all mediums seemed to be on the large side, my teacher told me with a roll of her eyes at my stupidity that it was were the Spirit world stored the ectoplasm... Yes I believed her.

One night when this student was in charge we did the meditation and once again asked us all what we got I was so embarrassed all I had in mine was a monkey laughing at me. So I took a breath and told her half turning away from me she said "that sounds about right for you", and that was the total of my explanation. Then something strange happened. We were all sitting listening to the student/teacher when I had this inexplicable feeling of being pushed out of my chair I could feel the chair tilting with me on it, could this be happening or was it my imagination? I looked behind me to see if any of the group were standing there which of course I knew they were not because they were all sitting in the circle listening like I was. I was so scared and cried out for the student teacher to help me. Could this be one of those evil spirits trying to enter me I wondered, had I not put my protection in place or opened my chakras properly? "Just say a prayer and tell them to leave you alone" which I promptly did reciting the Lord's Prayer, our Father who art in Heaven. Everyone in the group could hear the fear in my voice and my eyes filled with tears don't cry whatever you do don't cry I said to myself, but I was upset and I wanted to know what had happened but once again no explanation. Years later I found out it was the Spirit world trying to influence me to speak.

I should have walked away then but I didn't. I don't know but I felt the need to stay I am still not sure why, maybe it was all I had in my life that was mine and I didn't have to share with my husband or children. I had been controlled by my mother all my young life and then went into a marriage that controlled me so maybe this was mine, it belonged to me and no one could share it, maybe it had nothing to do with the Spirit world and developing at all just maybe my motives were more selfish than that.

The exercises continued week after week all were meant to connect us to the Spirit world but what had happened to me had unnerved me and I was more than a little scared to join in but if anyone noticed they never said anything, in fact that incident was never mentioned again. There were no words of reassurance or comfort, it was just swept under the carpet.

One exercise was psychometry this technique has been used for a long time, it works on the premise that all objects hold memories or vibrations of its owner's and that a sensitive can pick up on these vibrations. We had to bring in jewellery belonging to a dead person and place the jewellery anonymously on to a tray then we would choose an object hold it in our hands and feel the vibrations from it. I took along my mums necklace (she was always convinced the necklace was bad luck) a student picked it up "the person who owns this has been through some ups and downs in their life but the chain is long so it will get better". I grew more and more weary, does the Spirit world never say who they are do they only give information on our problems in life? I asked myself every night. Then one evening my prayers were answered the teacher told us to sit in pairs and to try and give a spirit link to our partner still no explanation how to, but it was a start. My friend Maureen started by describing her ex mother-in-law's home, "I can see the heavy velvet curtains and the big heavy table" My teacher was furious, "stop giving yourself a message Maureen and get on with it." When the teacher was out of ear shot, the lady Maureen was paired with said, "you have just described my grandmother's living room as I remember it". Maureen was so disappointed and it knocked her confidence badly.

This was the problem, our teacher was a wonderful medium, but had no idea about the mechanics of mediumship in short she didn't understand how it worked. No one ever told us that the Spirit world would use our own memories and experiences to get their message across. When I think back I cannot believe we put up with what we did what I thought was amazing was in fact nothing short of 'fumbling in the dark'. The two most bizarre things that happened I tell my students all the time to try and demonstrate my naivety.

The first was when we had to bring in photos of someone who has died, we had to put them in envelopes and cello taped them to our foreheads so we could get a better view through our third eye. Our teacher reliably informed us that she regularly did this when playing cards or held it to her solar plexus, and she always won. Well what more did I need to know, I did what was asked and concentrated really hard, all I got was a headache I still couldn't 'see' anything. I sometime wish we had photographed our exercises because of how bizarre they were.

The next was when I was asked to stand in front of the students, "ok Jackie I want you to get a link for someone in the room without looking so turn your back to the group". I was horrified, I struggled when I could see them so how would I ever manage if I couldn't, so I did the only thing I could I asked... "Please could you tell me how?" "For goodness sake Jackie it's always you, just turn your back throw your third eye over your head see who you want to give your message to and then bring your third eye back." How amazing is that? To be able to throw your third eye over your head I just had to master this, so for weeks I walked around practising flicking my third eye over my head until someone asked "excuse me but do you have Tourette's?"

Yes I really did this such faith I had in my teacher after all I had watched her delivering messages she could talk to Spirit so she must be right!

# Chapter 3.

## Progress at last

So the discerning reader may be able to tell that my early days in development were not the most enlightening for me, certainly not what I expected them to be., well that is not quite right, in truth I had no expectations this was all new to me so I did not know what I should expect, maybe if I had some prior knowledge I would not be so gullible.

Eventually things began to fall into place, still to this day I am not sure how but, one evening in our group the teacher informed me that the following Sunday I will be a taking my first Divine service with her., now I cannot stress to the reader what an honour it is to take a Divine service within our Spiritualist churches, just as it is for a Rabbi or priest. The Divine service is the most special night in our calendar and it is also the shop window were the public get to see what we Spiritualists are about.

I was elated, petrified, excited and shocked all at the same time. Me on the rostrum just like the medium predicted all those months ago. But very much aware also of the responsibility, so the pressure was also on my shoulders.

The days leading up to the Divine service went by in a blur what would I wear, what would I say, would anyone turn up, either living or dead. I was a mess; I had never experienced nerves like it.

I meditated every day, sometimes twice, I begged the Spirit world to show up, and more importantly made doubly sure my chakras were open and my cloak of protection was in place so no evil Spirits could take advantage of me.

I still did not know what I was opening after all these months (6 in total,) I was never told exactly what a chakra was or what its function was.

The Sunday arrived and it just happened to be harvest festival, this is a special service were we give thanks for the produce and food  Mother Nature has provided for us all year the church was packed to capacity, I thought I would die, or even worse take leave of my lunch on the churches new blue carpet.

A very tall lady introduced us (this lady became known to me as Big Bet, she died some years ago from Cancer, but a strict formidable lady who I don't think I ever saw smile) she made particular reference to how fortunate the church was to have such a wonderful medium, my teacher, in the church, then almost as an afterthought said and Jackie is a fledgling, [fledgling is a name giving to a trainee medium].

It didn't worry me I sat there on this raised platform looking out at a sea of expectant faces,  yes I was nervous, worried and scared but I truly felt as though I was home, something I had never felt even as a child, a sense of belonging. I can remember thinking to myself, if I never move from here I could die happy the first time in my life, I belonged.


 The Teacher rose to her feet and delivered her prayer, then we sang a hymn 'all things bright and beautiful' as we started the hymn, I give it all I had, until my teacher nudged me in the ribs and whispered, 'sit down and meditate do not sing again'. I have never been blessed with a goof singing voice even at school I was banned from the choir because the teacher said I was tone deaf.

Oh well not such bad advice I thought. Then it began, the mediumship.  My teacher gave three messages all taken and understood, the energy was high in the room and people were happy. Ok Jackie, now your turn, I stood and faced the congregation. "someone here has a Scottish connection," I said tentively a lady raised her hand, "you have a father in Spirit" "yes" came the broad Scottish reply, then nothing else, we had never been taught what to do after that first initial bit of information, everyone was looking at me and I didn't know what to do. "Oh he loves you very much". I said, remembering what the medium had said to me in my message all those months ago, and promptly sat down.

People nodded in approval and my teacher carried on, afterwards she said, "well done Jackie you can do it on your own next time". I nearly fainted I could never do a whole service not in a million years.

The next week at class the other students had heard about my apparent success, and with some their attitude towards me became hostile. I didn't know why, I had only given half a message. But other than that we went back to the same exercises, throwing our third eye, sticking envelopes to our heads, all the usual stuff that the Spirit world wanted us to do, or so we were lead to believe. It was impossible to see if this training was the same in other churches because we were banned from attending any other church, the rules were, if you were getting developed in this church you supported it on the Saturday night and did not go to any other, if you did you would be thrown out.

Then one evening I had gone to the class as always, by now I had many doubts in my mind, could mediumship really be that easy, was there not more to it?

This particular evening my husband came to collect me from class, he came in after the class had ended and my teacher commented that he looked tired. Now I feel I should give you a little extra information at this point, my then husband (we have since divorced) was a driver by profession who frequently drove long distances.

"Yes 'he replied 'it's been a long day, I have driven to Scotland and Back".

My teacher narrowed her eyes and placing a finger on her chin, began to slowly shake her head, oh no that is not the reason then slowly she walked around him, and then said very loudly to him "sit!" I could see the colour drain from his face as he looked towards me in an accusing way. But nobody disagreed with my teacher what she said you did and that is what my husband did, he timidly walked towards a chair and sat down, he looked like a rabbit caught in the head lights.

My teacher explained that the cause of his tiredness was because he had a Spirit trapped in his Aura, and this male Spirit was taking my husband's energy. "Come everyone let's get to work". And so it began rhythmically heave ho, heave ho, as my teacher walked around pulling at this Spirit until finally after a very long five minutes, she declared, 'it is done, he is free'.

Oh the relief, how wonderful that my teacher could do this, but it did not stop there, of course if she had freed a trapped Spirit then my husband would obviously have a gaping hole left in the energy field, so my teacher set about 'sewing up the hole' then smoothing down the frayed edges, until my husband's aura looked acceptable to this trained eye.

I would ask the reader at this point to try and remember that this is what I once believed, later in the book I will explain how my thoughts have changed, also that the 'sewing up' was done with an imaginary needle and thread.

This was probably the last straw, it didn't feel right to me and I could no longer go on without having explanations giving. My husband was very angry with me and pointed out that it was a place full of idiots that should be locked up, I felt hard pushed to disagree with him because this is exactly what I felt too. But before I could leave there was one more act of humiliation.

One day while at home the phone rang, "Jackie the medium has cancelled for Sunday, you are taking it" and before I could reply the phone went down.

It was Friday and the service was on Sunday oh God what was I to do. All too quickly the day came, I had not slept, I did not eat, and I stood in front of the mirror practising the talk I had to give. But generally feeling sick to the stomach.

The night came, now it was my turn to look like a rabbit caught in the glare of a cars headlights.

The very tall lady, Big Bet, introduced me again, as the teachers fledgling. And then handed the service over too me.

"Good evening" I stuttered "will you join me in Prayer", I rambled badly through the prayer, apologising to God under my breath, then forgot the talk I had rehearsed all day, and talked instead about my mums death I think the term is I winged it, badly.

Then came the mediumship, nothing, absolutely nothing happened, my teacher threw me one of her disappointed looks. 'Oh God take me now' I have never said so many prayers in my head so quickly, I all but stopped at selling my soul to the devil. If only someone would help me then suddenly within my head I could 'hear' some little boy saying mammy, "I have a young boy here, wants his Mam", a lady put up her hand, 'his head hurt' he tells me and he was in Hospital. (Once again I am still not sure how I got that information.) The lady started to cry, and nodded at me, that was it I had no more and sat down, I could not give any more messages I was finished. I was also very much aware of the disapproving looks I was getting, all those people all that expectation, and I had let them down.

That night I laid in bed and cried I had let everyone down, all those people who were hoping their family would show up and I had let them down, the responsibility was too much, that poor lady how many more was their like her, needing that hope and comfort.

I sent a letter the next day explaining I was very honoured to have been part of the group but it was not for me, and I would not be coming back.

Nobody tried to stop me.

I had spent a year trying to learn this thing called mediumship and in my mind I had failed.

I spent days after this trying to sort my feelings out I missed the group, but did I miss it for the right reasons? I kept in touch with Maureen who had also left by this time too.

Yet somehow I could not walk away completely.

One day I spoke to my brother Geoff about my grandmother, "can you tell me anything about her Mediumship" I asked.

"Not much, she lived in Motherwell close to Glasgow, where my dad and his brother Robert were born. She would hold meetings in her home, but at that time it was illegal so our older brother Bill would sometimes act as her look out, and if he saw the police he would bang on her door, and all her 'guests' would leave out of the back. But that is as much as I know". But this intrigued me, I had read a couple of books Doris stokes mainly and she had said in one of her books about mediumship being hereditary, so I thought maybe, just maybe I could have inherited her 'gifts'.

Some weeks later, I decided to try again, I went back to Boro Road Church, and I saw on the wall an advertisement for The Arthur Findlay College, what was this I wondered. So again I asked the president of the church he told me it was an elite college that trained mediums on residential courses, you lived in for a week or weekend and they helped you to understand mediumship, but it was a very long way and very expensive.

For the next 3 months I thought about it and thought about it, but because money was tight and my children were still very young, my daughters were at secondary school and Craig had just started primary not to mention that my husband usually said no to everything I asked I tried my best to put it out of my mind.

In Boro road Church they had for sale a weekly newspaper called the 'Psychic news' one evening I bought it and took it home, laid in bed reading it and once more there were articles and advertisements about this college.

I had to go, it became an itch I couldn't scratch, but how and what course? One thing was for sure if I went it could only be a weekend.

I carefully brought up the subject to my husband, he had never asked why I no longer went to church, and I didn't feel the need to explain.

"Did you know there is a college for Mediumship development" I asked one evening, no reply, "I think it would be good to go and have a look, what do you think?"

He looked up at me and said, "If you can find the money you can go".

I could not believe it, as long as I could find the money I could go, wow this was unheard of, I felt I was walking on a cloud, I could go. So how to find the money was my next challenge. I checked the courses and the only one I could afford and realistically go to was a course on Hypnosis and Mediumship; I liked the sound of that. (Did I know what hypnosis was? Not really).

My Uncle, my mum's brother lived alone in his own little flat, since mam had died, before that he had lived with us all my young life my uncle was our constant when we came home from school he was there and when we got up he was there with our breakfasts ready even though he was disabled, and had been since birth he was more capable of looking after us than our mam was. So I went and asked him, "Please could you lend me the money to go to this college?" "You're mad Jackie it will end in tears", he said as he handed me the money.

I was going to go to this strange college it was set, I talked to the kids they were ok about me going, but now it was a reality my husband was not happy he had not thought I would be able to raise the money. But I had and nothing would stop me, I was going to this strange college.

## Chapter 4

## The Arthur Findlay College.

The Arthur Findlay College is in the south of England close to Essex.

Built in 1871, Stansted hall was the home of Arthur Findlay MBE, an honorary president of the Union. He bequeathed the hall to the Spiritualist National Union in 1964 a year after the death of his wife. Findlay wrote several books on Spiritualism and psychic science which can still be bought today.

And it was my turn to go; I was like a child waiting for Christmas.

The course I was booked on was called hypnosis and Mediumship and the big day was here. Supplied with a map and a full tank of petrol I was ready to go, have I already said I was excited? Good because I was, I had this wonderful sense of freedom, what would it be like? Would it be full of Spirits? If so would they be disappointed because I had not yet mastered how to throw my third eye over my head?

I arrived late having taken a wrong turn, so tired and hungry I drove into the Driveway and followed a long road to the Entrance. Nothing had prepared me for the sight in front of me, a large Victorian house, standing tall in the fading light, I took in a sharp breath, and it was amazing, surrounded by trees and fields.

I unloaded my car and made my way to the front door, straight in front of me was the reception desk, I gave my name and the lady gave me my key to my room, "you have a room to yourself" she said, "the other person you were sharing the room with has cancelled". This was definitely meant to be. A very comfortable room 2 beds and a shower, once again that feeling of belonging swept over me. I couldn't wait till tomorrow.

It was a sleepless night so much going around in my head. But the morning came and I hurried down to breakfast, there was a large sweeping staircase that lead down to the long gallery, from there you could get access to the library and the large lounge and also the lecture hall, beautiful rooms with so much history.

Once in the dining room I was once again feeling like the new kid at school, everyone seemed to know each other so I sat quietly listening to the conversations. There were students from all over the world and they had all obviously been here many times before. One lady called Petra from Germany said to me, "you must see the gardens they are so beautiful". I was so enchanted by this magnificent place I honestly never wanted to leave.

Then the first lesson, we all had to meet in the library, A beautiful room with wall to wall bookcases, all packed with old books, to be honest I could have spent the entire weekend looking through the books I have always had a fascination for books. On the walls were pictures of three men I was later to discover these were, Minister Eric Hatton, Minister Hatton is a past president of the Spiritualist National Union and a much loved and respected gentle man. Albert Best a very famous medium and the famous medium, teacher and president of the Spiritualist National Union Gordon Higginson, none whom I had heard of at the time. The day started. The teachers were a man and a woman, the group was divided into two and we were giving the rules of the course, one was, there will be absolutely no private sittings on this course as we have not enough time to do them and the students are forbidden to give sittings to each other.

I have to admit I was lost, lots of technical jargon that I had never heard before, and no mention of protection or opening up.

The weekend passed very quickly the actual course was not very inspiring, and once again ended up with me being the butt of the teacher's jokes. You see I have a habit of asking the stupid questions, one day I will learn to just shut up.

On the Saturday I asked the question could everyone be hypnotised. Simple enough question you would think.

The teacher listened to my question and told me to come to the front and sit on the therapy bed he had waiting. He then started to ask me questions, "are you enjoying the college"? Did you enjoy breakfast? I nodded enthusiastically, then without warning he put his hand over my face and said loudly "sleep". I was aware of his voice somewhere around me but could not wake up. I have never been so afraid in all my life. After that he 'brought me back' but for the rest of the day he would randomly shout, sleep, and I would. (Note to student, find out about the persons back ground before doing this) I had an abused childhood so this feeling of being rendered helpless sent me into panic and I could not wait to return home, not to mention lunch time when he shouted across the dining room, "SLEEP", and I ended up with shepherd's pie all over my brand new trousers.

My drive home give me a lot of time to think, I had so very much enjoyed been in the beautiful surroundings of the college, but it had also left me with a lot more questions.

It would be a whole year before I returned to the college, I saved up my spare money and paid to go on a week of mediumship with a tutor named Glyn Edwards. This man changed my life forever, since beginning this book Glyn has passed away to Spirit, such a sad loss for all who knew him.

If you have not met Glyn before he is a man with a lot of wisdom and knowledge and it was he who give me my first real teaching in mediumship I longed for the mornings to come when we would all sit in the sanctuary of the college and listen to Glyn's words. The practical training was common sense, never once did he tell me to use protection or open chakras or throw my third eye over my head. Instead he talked about a world of love and intelligence that has a natural order; he told us you could *ask* the Spirit world to join you. (Now to you students that might sound silly but after my first training this was such a revelation.) Glyn was the first teacher that told me about the importance of sitting in the power, a practice I still do to this very day and I encourage all my students to do this too. (Later in the book I will explain this technique.)

Glyn's weeks became my yearly holiday. I saved every spare penny I had to be able to go on his weeks; I met fantastic teachers, and learnt so much about the Spirit world and mediumship. I do not have the words here to say how much I valued Glyn as a medium and a teacher and I will be ever grateful he put me on the right path.

I had refused to take another service until I could be sure that I could work correctly, I practised prayer and mediumship as much as I could and eventually began taking services again. My children became my congregation, listening to my endless philosophies and prayers until I got it right and believe me I am still trying to get it right.

It was not long before my reputation began to grow and I got an invite to work in Northern Ireland, and a place I still love, the warmth of the people is unbelievable and I call it my second home.

I was then encouraged to become a member of the SNU (Spiritualist National Union) and apply for my certificate in demonstrating, I didn't think I stood a chance; I had never had any schooling how was I going to cope with the course work? But I did cope and I decided I would have a week at the college to sharpen my mediumship up a bit in preparation, this time it was not Glyn's week but another teacher I had a good week, but the teacher I was put with didn't seem to like me very much (or am I being over sensitive?) at the end of the week as we sat in the magnificent sanctuary, the 'church' of the college where the demonstrations of mediumship and the services were held, the teacher give each student a quick assessment on what she had seen, each one she said how wonderful they had worked, and how impressed she was with their work.

She did not say a word to me; I felt my stomach drop, all my insecurities from my childhood bounced back into my head and heart, "you are just not good enough Jackie" my old voices in my head screamed at me. So I asked her, "Please could I just ask, I have an assessment on Saturday for my certificate in demonstrating, do you think I will do ok?"

The pitying look rolled over her face "No you have no chance of passing, your Mediumship is not good enough" came the reply.

I cried all the way home, but it was too late to cancel the assessment, Saturday came, I woke up, and my son had put post-it notes on all the doors and cupboards, what date was Hydesville? Who were the fox sisters? Every question from my SD1 was positioned around my home bless him no wonder he is such a great school teacher now.

I went along to my assessment in a local church, knowing I would fail, after all that's what the teacher had said after all she was a teacher of the Arthur Findlay College so she had to be right.

"Jackie we are pleased to tell you, you have passed your certificate in demonstrating". They then went on to say, "That was a fine demonstration and we were all very impressed well done." The tears streamed down my face but this time with pride and happiness.

This is a huge lesson to all students, teachers no matter how good they are, are only human, put them in charge of your life and you will end up disappointed.

But despite this, The Arthur Findlay College is truly a college of excellence and I have been privileged to work with some of the finest mediums.

Eamonn Downey, probably the best metaphysical teacher that has ever lived, his unique way of seeing just what the student needs to bring out the best in them, and he is unique in the way he encourages the student to work on themselves not just their mediumship. I have often said to him I should pay him when I work on his weeks because I learn so much about me.

Paul Jacobs, probably one of the finest clairvoyants there has ever been. Paul was the first medium to ever give me an accurate message from my mother. Some 32 years after her death, in the college, Paul described very accurately mam's illness her death and subsequently her growth within the Spirit world. In that one message Paul showed me the healing power of mediumship and lifted a huge weight off my shoulders. The three men I have mentioned, Eamonn Paul and Glyn, I owe a great deal too. All have shown me kindness and wisdom in different ways, I feel very privileged to have been associated with them.

Years later I was to become a tutor at this fine college, yet another journey that showed me the fallibility of people and that insecurity was not a burden only I had to bear.

A very wise man said to me, "there are no evil people but there are damaged people".

I learnt that people are people no matter what their 'gift's May be.


I, now in my assessments for students refuse to say whether they can be mediums or not, I believe fully that this is a contract they have between themselves and the Spirit world, after all I am only human which makes me fallible.

I also do not like teaching advanced mediumship, for two reasons, if I teach advanced mediumship it implies I am more advanced than the advanced, which can never be true. Also if the student thinks they are advanced then why are they still relying on a physical teacher? Why are they not going to their teachers in the Spirit world for advice?

This was a small glimpse into my journey in to mediumship, the next part of this book is a practical guide to assist the student on their journey.

# CHAPTER 5.

## TIPS FOR THE STUDENT,

The point of this book was not just to tell you about my life or early development. It was to try and ask the student to keep an open mind and not to be afraid to question everything. On the next few pages I would like to share some practical advice on your actual development.

Every student I believe, should begin by looking at their reasons for wanting to be a medium a little while ago I asked some students this question and one actually replied, "I want to be on the telly and earn big money". Now I do not have a problem with mediums being on the TV or earning a living but, if this is your only reason I don't believe it will get you very far. I always say to students examine your motive and reasons, but the Spirit world know what is in your heart, they will know the true motive.

Try to remember working as a medium is a wonderful ability but it is hard work you have to have a heightened sense of responsibility. You are constantly dealing with people's grief and facing the prejudices of people's lack of understanding. You keep unsociable hours and spend many days away from your family so in some respects it can be quite lonely too. So try to keep your feet on the ground and be realistic. I was once advised to only work 2 Sundays in every month, but that went out the window when I came up against booking secretaries who are quite pushy, it is important you try to balance your working time with your family time.

**Begin at the beginning.**

Where I feel we have gone wrong over the years with the training of our student mediums, is in the way we bombard the student with exercises a lot of the time without even asking if the student understands the exercise, and the reason we are doing it. It seems we have developed a culture of keep the student busy at all costs without any real understanding of what it should accomplish.

We have forgotten or neglected to teach the student how to sit for Spirit. To sit for no other reason but to learn how it feels when the Spirit world is around you, to allow the Spirit world their time to adjust to the student we mistakenly think it is all about us, when in the back ground the Spirit world are learning how best to blend with the medium and understand the medium's energy. I believe that the majority of medium's especially new mediums on our rostrums do not understand when they are working with the Spirit world and when they are working with the energy of the congregation.

So I ask students every day to 'sit in the power'. This is a technique that was given to Glyn Edwards by the Spirit world during a trance demonstration.

This technique has very little to do with the Spirit world but is an exercise to build up the 'power' of the medium so the Spirit world can gain a greater blend with the medium.

How many times do we hear a medium begin a message with "I have your father here he died of a heart attack", and then starts to talk about your life and what you are doing and there is no more evidence from Dad. That for me shows that the medium has not worked on their own energy field and so cannot hold the mind of the Spirit long enough to get good evidence from them. If we understand the route of the message we know that the Spirit's mind blends with the mediums mind to deliver the message in a telepathic way, but we also know that the journey to the mediums mind is via the mediums auric field.

So the stronger the aura the stronger the blend.

I do this exercise every morning without fail, so I know what a difference it will make to your mediumship.

### Sitting in the power.

This is a very easy technique and can be done anywhere any time.

Sit quiet and focus on your breath. Imagine that there is a small light in the centre of your chest. With each in breath the light gets bigger, with each out breath the light gets brighter.

Do this until the light completely envelopes you, until the light and you are one with no separation. Then imagine you are forcing the light out till it touches every wall around you. Use your mind to make this happen.

Next invite the Spirit world to draw close, don't look for names or descriptions, but learn to recognise their presence, the feelings they bring around you when they are present.

Practice this every chance you get, it is not difficult, complicated or dangerous, but it is invaluable to your mediumship. I call it 'laying the foundations'. We would not build a house without first ensuring the foundations were in place. So the same applies to your mediumship, this is your workout in preparation for the communication.

Remember, that your mind will fight for supremacy when you close your eyes, it will recreate colours and images and symbols. It will remind you that you have left the door unlocked or the phone is going to ring, this is normal, your brain is doing its job. So don't fight it, you will not win. Instead gently encourage it to watch your breath, eventually it will give up and slow down, then in that space the Spirit world can draw close without interference.

In the days of old, mediums would sit and sit, not doing exercises but just waiting for the touch of Spirit and once they recognised that presence then the communication could begin. Today we tend to do it the other way around, we do exercise after exercise but never fully recognise when the Spirit world is present.

So let's begin at the beginning and sit just for Spirit. Let's learn to understand their touch and what they want from us.


I heard a lovely story about Fanny Higginson (Gordon Higginson's mum).

I was told that potential mediums would have to sit for up to two hours once a week in a dark room, without speaking, until they could recognise when Spirit was present then and only then could the student progress to another group.

We have lost this art, we now want our mediumship instantly and in my opinion this is very wrong.

So let's begin at the beginning and get it right here, and then we can move on to the next step.

## Chapter 6.

## MOVING ON.

Have we got the foundations right? Good, then let's move on.

When I was developing the word psychic was an unspoken word, as though somehow it was contaminated. But it is important that the student exercises and strengthens their psychic ability. Learning to recognise when you are working with the energy of a living person is as important as knowing the Spirit world.

There are hundreds of techniques for improving psychic energy. But why not make it fun, invite your friends around for a psychic night and practice with, things like coloured ribbons or papers. Ask one of your friends to choose three colours, one colour relates to their emotional energy, one to their mental and one to their spiritual, give them a reading from this, then progress to past, present and future.

I like to collect photographs out of magazines, and put them onto card, I would ask a friend to pick a card and then I would do a reading from the picture. Of course the picture has no magic powers; it is a focus so you and your sitter relaxes. When they are relaxed their energy field opens up and you can feel the information more clearly. The picture also stimulates your 'feeling mind', your intuition.

 Don't get hung up on what others are doing. Find what is comfortable for you. Remember you are unique, don't become a copy of someone else. Working psychically is about working with your feelings, your intuition. We all wear a mask that hides the 'real us'. Try to discover what is behind your friend's mask. But always be kind and responsible. Remember you are working with another human being, don't try to be clever by uncovering their hidden or painful past.

But working this way can be fun and informative, why not ask your friends to bring a friend so you are working with people you know nothing about? Strengthen this aspect of you by becoming a people watcher, when you are sitting in a café for example, ask yourself what does the person on the next tables energy speak to me about.

When you recognise this energy of the psychic, you will more easily recognise the difference of the energy of the Spirit world. So many students say to me, I don't know if it is me or Spirit? That's because they have not took the time to work on both energies till they know the difference.

A point to consider, if you are going to do private sittings, then you will not only have people who want a Spirit contact, you will have people needing guidance on their marriage, job or finance. It is then you will work more with their energy than Spirits. So it is important that you perfect this.

There are the old techniques that really are the best. Try asking yourself who is phoning you, and who has sent the letter to you, before you look at the number or the post mark. If you are on a bus or in your car, what vehicle is behind you, you will be amazed how quickly you start to get things right.

Once again make it fun, development should be an enjoyable journey.

## Getting Serious.

There are lots of exercises that a student can use but the best are the ones that deprive you of your physical senses; using blind folds may be old, but it is still one of the best ways. As we cancel out our sight we strengthen our inner vision.

**Psychometry** is a good way of feeling energy and recognising emotions. Everything in the Universe is surrounded by a magnetic field that radiates its own special vibration. In Psychometry we utilise this when we touch or hold an object that belongs to someone else. A psychometrist, whilst holding a ring, for instance, is able to pick up the combined vibrations of both the ring and its owner. This is because when an object is worn or carried for some time it will absorb the owner's psychic energy (vibrations).

You may find it hard to believe but you have been using psychometry all your life, for example when you shake hands with somebody you may suddenly get an impression or feeling about them, The moment you come into contact with an object a two way process of energy exchange takes place naturally. To become a good psychometrist you have to learn to become sensitive to the vibrations coming from the object.

### How to begin with psychometry.

1. Start with an object that has been owned by somebody for more than a year, the item can be anything, jewellery, ornaments but silver or gold is best.
2. Relax as much as you can, follow your breath, prepare yourself before you pick up the object.
3. Pick up your item, hold it comfortable and 'feel it' get used to its texture and shape but try not to analyse or expect anything.
4. Take a deep breath and start to say what you feel or see, don't worry about what you are saying or worry about whether it makes sense and don't try too hard.
5. Ask the owner of the item for feedback and don't be put off if you don't get it completely right first time.
   In the beginning you will probably pick up the emotional parts of the object's history, consequently you will pick up feelings of illness, emotional problems, past and present, please do not be put off by this but look for the positive. It is also good to practice with photographs of people you don't know, just follow the same steps as above.

### PSYCHIC AIDS.

It is useful in the beginning to use an 'aid' to help you link into your subject psychically.

When practising with readings, you may help the process by using psychometry to pick up on your client's problems and use precognition to help forecast the trends in your client's life. All of this will be helped with the use of an aid. Below are a few examples of what the novice can use to heighten their sensitivity.

*Tarot cards.*

No one really knows were Tarot cards originated from, the oldest deck still in existence was made for Charles VI of France and dates back to 1392. Through the ages they have been banned accused of being the devils cards or tied in with witch craft. But when you take the superstition away the Tarot are a valuable tool for increasing ones sensitivity. The packs usually contain 78 cards – 22 Major Arcana and 56 Minor Arcana. If you are interested in trying these most packs come with an explanation book, but it is worth spending time feeling the energy of each card and getting your own impressions of each one.

*Runes.*

The Runes have enjoyed an upsurge of popularity in the recent years. Their origin is attributed to both the Celts, the Norse and the Anglo Saxons. Runes became popular in England in the fifth century, but where used in Sweden and Germany long before then. The word is derived from *ru,* Germanic for secrecy, and *runa,* Gothic for mystery. Usually comprising of 25 stones each Rune has its own meaning; 1. Communication. 2, Partnership, 3. Signals Good advice. 4. Retreat, inheritance. 5. Strength, good fortune. 6. Initiation. 7. Restraint Caution. 8. Fertility. 9. Defence. 10. Spirit. 11. Possessions. 12. Joy. 13. Harvest. 14. Relationships. 15. Love affair. 16. Unity. 17. Changes. 18. Inspiration, 19. Disruption. 20. Journey. 21. Good fortune. 22. Ambition. 23. Indifference. 24. Decision. 25. Destiny.

There are many many other aids you can use. It is about experimenting and finding which one is right for you. Crystals, flowers the crystal Ball. Sand and water. All have been used for many years but can be both fun and useful in increasing your sensitivity.

A useful aid is ESP cards:

Serious scientific investigation into ESP began as far back as 1915 at Stanford University, but the momentum really began when Duke University opened up a parapsychology laboratory under the direction of Dr. J. B. Rhine in the early 1930's.

What is ESP, ESP stands for extra sensory perception, and it comes under the branch of parapsychology which specialises in psychical research. The whole field is called PSI it is a term used by parapsychologists and refers to all kinds of psychic phenomena and is divided into two parts: ESP and psychokinesis (PK) ESP can be defined as the ability to obtain knowledge by extra sensory rather than sensory means. PK is the ability to influence an object or event. Mind over matter.

One of their inventions was to develop a special pack of cards for testing psychic abilities. This deck was originally called Zenner cards and it consisted of 25 cards, 5 different symbols repeated five times each. (Circle, wavy lines, star, square and plus sign.)They were used to determine someone's ability at telepathy, clairvoyance and precognition. Here is one of the tests for Clairvoyance.

1. Sit comfortably with your cards paper and pen.
2. Shuffle the cards thoroughly and place them face down on the table.
3. Take the top card off the deck, holding it so you cannot see what is on it.
4. Write down what you think the card is.
5. You can continue in two different ways from this point. You can look at the card to see if you are correct, then move onto the next one or you can continue all the way through the deck, and check your success at the end.
6. The chance score is five correct out of 25 cards, (20%) If you can consistently do better than this average then you are successfully demonstrating your clairvoyant abilities.

    You can change this by using two people. One person visualises the card and 'sends' it to the psychic who writes down the image, this will strengthen your telepathy.

    To test your precognition, Mix the cards and then 'guess' the identity of the card that will come up, for example you may see the star card, and when you pick up the cards it is the star that turns up.

    Clairvoyance. Ask someone to thoroughly mix up the cards and then place them into a box or envelope. Relax, then try to clairvoyantly identify the top card of the deck, write it down, then the same with the second and third. Until you have gone right through the deck.

Precognition. Remove one each of the 5 symbols and place them to one side. Divide the remaining cards into 5 piles, each containing one symbol (one pile has four circles, one has four stars etc.) Place the five piles in order from your left to right where you think the 5 cards you previously removed will go. Once this has been done, determine where the remaining 5 cards will go in the following manner; the circle relates to 1 and 2, the 'plus' sign to 3 and 4, the wavy line to 5 and 6, the square to 7 and 8 and the star to 9 and 0 Open up a telephone directory to any page and look at the last digit of the first entry on that page. If it is a 1 place the circle on top of your first pile of cards, if it is a 5 you would place the wavy lines repeat this 4 more times then check to see if you have managed to successfully predetermine the correct spot for each pile.

The area of ESP can be divided into a number of sub categories:

TELEPATHY. This is the ability to send and receive thoughts. Mind reading, If I am thinking about something and you pick up my thought it would be an example of telepathy.
PSYCHOMETRY. The ability to get feeling from an object or place whilst holding or touching it.

PRECOGNITION (OR PREMONITION) The ability to foretell the future if you had a strong impression or feeling that a certain event was going to occur say in the next month, and it actually happened then that would be an example of precognition.

But with all of this, it is important to remember that it all takes practice. And nothing is achieved over night, so if your results are not instant keep trying.

# Chapter 7.

## THE NEXT STEP.

Now we have understood the psychic element we will on to the mediumship

What does mediumship mean? Well it is the ability to communicate with another mind, to gain information that can be identified by the recipient as evidence. We are told that there are numerous senses that a medium works through.

*Clairvoyance;* clear seeing, the ability to see the Spirit world and accurately describe them to their loved ones.

*Clairaudience;* clear hearing, the ability to hear the Spirit worlds words, accent and even if the Spirit world has a speech impediment etc.

*Clairsentience;* clear feeling, the ability to feel the Spirit world and to understand their character through feelings.

There are other senses too, but personally I do not think these really exist. I believe the only sense that really exists is Clairsentient. I believe that everything happens through the feeling Mind, the Spirit blends with the mind of the medium and the mediums brain tries to make sense of what it is experiencing so it changes the feeling to an audio or visual depending on the mediums natural ability. If the blend is successful then it may appear to the medium that they are 'hearing' the voice of Spirit, or 'seeing' the Spirit person.

The biggest problem every trainee medium will have, is keeping their mind focused on the energy around them. Let's try it for a moment.

Close your eyes and visualise a rainbow, hold that image for 20 seconds....

How did you do? I would expect, even in that short time, your mind had at least 3 other images that came in and out.

So imagine trying to hold the energy of the Spirit for 10 minutes or more, it is not easy.

So we need to find a way to keep your mind focused and stop it hopping about from image to image.

I said earlier about the value of your breath, if you can use your breath to calm the mind, it can be an extremely valuable tool.

You don't have to breathe deeply or hyper ventilate. Just breath naturally in your own rhythm, and eventually your brain will slow down and the random images will slow down also.

Pick an image like a rainbow or a rose and set the timer on your mobile for 30 seconds. Practice holding that image without your ego interrupting, once you can do this increase it to 60 seconds.

So we have built our power, we have recognised the presence of the Spirit, now let's get to know their story.

Try to remember the Spirit world wants you to know their story. They have chosen you to be the narrator of their story. They do not make it hard but we do. I have quite a structured and orderly mind, I want my messages to be structured too. I dislike it when a message jumps from this information to that.

So I always present my message in the following way;

Gender/Relationship.

Death/illness

Personality,

Family, work.

Memories.

Something the Spirit has seen their loved ones doing recently.

Reason for coming.

I believe we get who we need from Spirit not necessarily who we want.

You will notice I have not included descriptions; this is because I don't waste time on what are usually general descriptions if an average message from a platform is around 7 minutes, why would 'dad' waste time talking about his average height or weight? Surely he would want to get to the important information as quickly as possible.

So unless they had something unusual about their appearance like a false limb or wore a wig, unless they had a particular item of dress I don't bother seeking the obvious; it wastes valuable time and energy when we could be finding out the uniqueness of the person.

Sit with someone you love or know very well ask them to imagine they are in the Spirit world, now ask them to give you 3 things about themselves that they would tell a medium, I will guarantee they will not say their height, hair colour or their address or age.

They will talk about memories their job or their personality. Those in the Spirit world are no different, only after they have got their essence across to the medium will they then talk about the boring bits like their address or their names etc.

But don't believe me, test it for yourself.

I want you to remember that the role of the medium is to give evidence, and the Spirit world KNOW what evidence the sitter wants to hear, so get into your power, and let the Spirit world guide you.

### Experiment for beginners.

In the beginning it can be difficult to know how to start, so I use this exercise for the trainee who is just starting out to help them make their link. I am going to use a fictitious person so you will understand the process.

"Ok Sarah I am going to help you to make a link, just focus on your breath to begin with and I want you to look at the wall in front of you.' 'Sarah I want you to imagine that you are in your own home right now, can you do that easily?"

Sarah, "Yes I can"

"Great what room is your favourite?"

Sarah, 'Living Room'

'Ok I want you to imagine you are sitting in your living room on your favourite chair, I want you to understand that you are completely alone, and no one is going to disturb you. What is your favourite TV programme?'

Sarah, "A Documentary".

"Ok you have 10 minutes until that begins, so get comfy in your chair, now as you look towards the door, you are aware of a Spirit person standing in your door way, you don't know them they are a complete stranger, I want you to tell me when you know if it is male or female."

Sarah, "Male"

"That's great, now I want you to ask him to come a sit with you, can you do that,"

Sarah, "Yes I have done that."

"Ok how has he responded, has he come over quickly, or slowly?"

Sarah, "Slowly".

"Why do you think that is, is he bad on his legs, or is he shy?"

Sarah, "he seems to have problems with his legs"

I would then continue to offer questions to Sarah until we have built up a complete profile, relationship, death condition, personality etc.

If we were in a workshop or seminar, at the end I would ask to Sarah "who do you think he belongs too"?

By putting the trainee in her own environment she will feel empowered and not as on her own through the process. It is long and you will need patience but it also helps the trainee to formulate questions to ask the Spirit world.

**Clairvoyance exercise.**

Close your eyes get yourself comfortable, I want you to 'see' a rose, what does it look like? Does it have a colour? Is it fully bloomed or a tight bud?

Look at every detail be observant. Where do you see it? Is it in your mind's eye or is it a knowing rather than a seeing? It is easier for your brain to recreate an image that is known to you than an unknown image. For example, if I asked you to see a calabash, would you be able to 'see' this in your mind if you didn't know what it was. Try it what does your mind create from this word.

**Clairaudient exercise.**

Sit comfortably and focus on your breath to relax your mind

I want you to hear the sound of rain on a roof top listen to it as it drops onto the tiles of the roof. Where do you hear it? Is the sound in your ears? Next listen to the sound of the voice of a loved one who is still alive, remember the last conversation you had with them. Once again where do you hear the voice, is it in your mind, your heart our externally in your ears?

Clairaudience is often, wrongly assumed, to be an external sound, but it isn't always, when the medium has the right blend, they connect so closely to the Spirit person that all their memories are released into the mediums mind. The dialect and if the Spirit person has any speech impediments. All of this becomes known to the medium, but it is an inner knowing not necessarily an external sound. But as I keep repeating it is all to do with the blending the medium can obtain with the Spirit mind.

**Exercise for Clairsentience.**

Once again sit comfortably, focus as always on your breath allow the mind relax.

I would like you to taste a piece of chocolate in your mouth, and feel it beginning to melt in your mouth. How does it feel as it melts over your tongue? Can you taste the chocolate?

Once again where is the taste coming from?

This exercise helps you to recall the memory of chocolate and as you brain recreates this feeling your senses start to react to that memory, whether you like chocolate or not. Did you gulp at the thought of the chocolate melting over your tongue? Did you salivate when the chocolate stuck to the roof of your mouth?

## Chapter 8.

## Mediumship

One of the biggest problems with mediumship, is the medium, your biggest challenge is holding the energy of the Spirit person and not allowing your mind to wander away and so begin to create its own story, one of fantasy.

The medium needs to learn how to hold on to the link and follow the Spirit person's story. This is not always easy as the natural thing to do is to become involved in what is happening. Also when we recognised similarities with our own lives we start then to interfere.

There are a number of good exercises you can do to improve your concentration, I personally like this one when it is done in a form of meditation.

Sit comfortably, where you know you will not be disturbed, there are no hard and fast rules on sitting as long as your body is upright and comfortable.

Imagine you are in a field and it is a beautiful day, the sun is shining and there is a slight warm breeze.

As you sit on the grass, you can see a hot air balloon descending from the sky; it comes to a stop near to where you are sitting.

I want you to carefully climb in side, as you settle into this large and comfortable basket, the balloon starts to rise into the sky once more, carrying you high above the trees, how do you feel?

It takes you over a street that is very familiar to you, you can recognise your home. How does it look form this perspective?

Take a good look at your home, what do you recognise that you may not have noticed before? Is there a garden? Is there a car in the drive? What can you see? Do not allow you mind to wander to the neighbour's house or the surroundings. Just focus on your own home.

Now the Balloon starts to move once more, you now find yourself above your childhood home. What can you see? Look at this home, remember how it felt to live here, who also lived here with you?

This exercise is very much about observing with detachment, learning to see but not becoming involved. The Spirit and the sitter do not need you to be involved, just the bridge that can connect the two elements, so don't make it about you and your issues or pain.

A lot of Students say to me that they don't have a church or a group to go to,

My reply is always, create one. If you are interested then it is a safe bet other people are too, even if there are only two of you it is a start. Begin with a meditation circle get the blend right then progress from there, if you are willing the Spirit world will help to make it happen.

Most mediums suffer or have suffered with depression. I have read about and spoke with a lot of mediums and healers who talk about this part of them. Emma Hardinge Britton, probably the greatest trance Speaker ever and the lady who helped the Spiritualist National Union obtain the 7 principles, said that as a child she suffered with Melancholy. I think the reason for this is twofold, we all have issues within our lives or experiences that have in a way left its scar, this has to be looked at and dealt with if not it will affect your mediumship and hold you back. Secondly I believe we all have a magnetic energy within our Aura that needs to be used and when it is not used it stagnates and causes us to feel low or depressed. I certainly know it is true of me at the time of writing this I have taking a 3 week break and already I can feel that need to connect to Spirit and feel their presence around me. I use an analogy with students that I teach I say to them;

We are all 'cracked' in some way, that's why we are doing this work. The Spirit do not choose perfect vessels, they choose the ones that know life and the pain of life. For it is through the cracks the light can shine in. but you must work with that pain understand it and use it, not allow it to eat you up with bitterness and resentment.

So take time not just to develop your mediumship but to develop your own self too this should be a journey into your own Soul and not just a connection with Spirit.

It could be also that on this journey your relationship with people around you changes you may 'outgrow' some people, don't fight this or worry about it change is an inevitable part of life. Even Mother Nature discards the old to make way for the new learn to flow with nature and not fight the inevitable.

# Chapter 9

## Mediumship and its many facets.

There are many types of mediumship that can be confusing for the trainee. So let's try and go through some of the terminology and what they mean.


## Psychic and the Aura.

This is where we become aware of the living energy, so we read the information from the persons auric field, or an object like a ring for example. Everything retains information and by using our sensitivity we can obtain very good information. The Aura is an invisible body of energy that surrounds all living things, just as no two people are the same, no two auras are alike. At one time only psychics could see the aura, but in 1908 Dr. Walter J. Kilner discovered he could see auras by looking at them through a screen of dicyanin. This had the effect of making someone who looked through it temporarily short sighted, and therefore more able to see the radiation present in the ultra-violet part of the spectrum. In 1911 he published a book called 'the human atmosphere'. A revised edition was published in 1920 as 'The Human Aura.' Dr. Kilner claimed no psychic powers and insisted that anyone could see the Aura. In 1939 Semyon Dvidovich accidently discovered what is now known as Kirlen photography. If you place your finger in a Kirlen device the resulting photograph will show an array of colours around your finger. One fascinating aspect of these photographs is that a picture of a diseased leaf show a completely different type of aura than that of a healthy leaf. This raises a possibility of Aura healing.

The Aura is made up of several layers (we don't really know how many, it varies from 7 to 28) but each layer represent us in some way; the physical layer which remains close to the body, it tells a good psychic all about the person and their physical self the body bone structure organs etc. the mental layer all about the person on a mental level, how they are academically or if they have had any mental health issues. The emotional layer, how this person interacts with people emotionally are they open and accepting of people or are they closed and private? Spiritual layer which we are told can extend the furthest of all layers without restriction and it is this layer the Spirit world use as the vehicle to reach the medium's mind. This layer speaks to us of the person's Spiritual development or lack of it.  The aura cannot predict the future it can only hold information that has already happened I do not believe the Aura can become damaged or needs cleaning (more on that in the next chapter) nor do I believe an Aura is good or bad, it is only energy.

There are a number of ways to 'see' the Aura without a camera,

### METHOD 1.

Sit down in a straight backed chair with your feet on the floor and your hands resting on your thighs. Relax as much as you can, remember your breath for relaxing, then close your eyes. After focusing on your breath for a few minutes, picture in your mind's eye a close friend or family member, see what the person is wearing, what they are doing, don't rush this, take your time. Once you have a complete picture of this person in your mind, imagine this person has an aura around them. Don't hurry just let it happen, don't expect certain colours to be there and keep practising it.

Once you have mastered this method, try it out on someone. Sit down opposite someone, close your eyes and relax by following your breath. When you open your eyes do not look directly at the person in front of you but over their shoulder and allow your gaze to soften, you will see the aura around their head.

### METHOD 2.

This is simpler and quicker but not as accurate. You simply unfocus your eyes, look at the person in front of you, keep your sight unfocused and you will see the aura slightly fuzzy and blurry, once again it will appear white but with practice colours will come.

## METHOD 3.

You can do this alone or with a friend. Place your forefingers together against a dark background and then slowly move your fingers apart. You will notice rays of light usually white or grey, moving from one hand to another. Once you do it with your forefingers, try the whole hand. An interesting experiment is to try it with someone you don't get along with, this is interesting as Aura repel as well as attract. It is a fact that when around people or situations that make us uncomfortable our auras shrink and when we are with friends and loved ones our aura will expand.

We all know books that explain the meaning of colours of the aura but I urge you to find your own meaning. Every colour has a positive and negative meaning. For example, we could look at black and say it means, repulsion and negative energy, or we can look at it and say, strong and independent. So decide for yourself what you feel when you 'see' a colour.

## Mental Mediumship.

 Mental mediumship is the ability to link to a discarnate mind, a so called 'dead person'.

What we know is the Spirit world can communicate with us here on earth by using the mediums, the Spirit person can and does give evidence of their continued life and evidence of their life when on earth. The medium will have developed their clairvoyance, clairsentience or clairaudience, one or a mixture of the three.

This is sometimes also known as second hand mediumship because the Spirit has to connect first to the medium then the medium has to put those thoughts into word, this means there is always a danger of the medium distorting what the Spirit really wants to convey. This is also why it is a discipline, the medium needs to discipline their mind to stay with and follow the story of the Spirit person.

**Trance.**

Trance mediumship also comes under the heading of mental mediumship, the Spirit world still use the mind of the medium to deliver their words however the degree of blending is usually far greater than with the communication I have mentioned earlier.

Trance can take a long, long time to develop successfully and requires a great deal of patience and commitment from the medium. In my opinion the greatest use of trance is in two ways. Firstly to bring a stronger healing energy and secondly to obtain the guidance and information from the Guides and Higher minds. Trance Healing was very popular in the 1800s and the 1970s it declined somewhat in the 1990s but is now making a resurgence. The healer is in a much more passive state, which means the Spirit doctors can make a more direct link to the patient.

Speaking, the greatest information we have today about the Spirit world and what happens at the point of death has come to us from the teachings in trance. Again the medium needs to be in a passive state so the mind of the teacher in Spirit, sometimes called a guide, can be in harmony with the medium, and the Spirit guide can then pass through the mind of the medium the teachings or inspirational words they want to deliver. Trance is a very beautiful and important energy within our mediumship but it has to be done correctly. If the medium is truly being influenced by a discarnate mind their words and mannerisms should also be different from the medium's norm, more importantly the people present should be able to feel the presence of another mind. The Spirit world never enter the medium this is impossible to do, it is a co-operation between the mind of the medium and the mind of Spirit.

In my opinion, trance can be the most fraudulent discipline of mediumship though this fraud is not always intentional, it is usually because the medium is badly trained. If this is something you would like to do then learn as much as you can about what trance is and is not then be prepared to sit for the Spirit world so they can get the blend right.

My first experience of trance came at the Arthur Findlay College completely by accident. I was in a group with the late Muriel Tennant and she asked us to enter the trance states. I just thought I will close my eyes and she would not notice me. But I could hear someone calling my name, my conscious mind followed the voice and the next thing I knew was people where telling me how wonderful the words where. I was completely unaware of what had taken place, but since then I do understand that the Spirit world took an opportunity to show me what could happen if I allowed it. I think that is one of the obstacles with trance and that is 'surrendering' to the power. There is also the belief that if we are really in trance then we should have no memory of what was said. This is not true, we have to remember that the Spirit world use our brain to activate the vocal chords to enable words to be spoken, so therefore it is logical that our brain has to be active to a point, so we will always have an awareness.

There is a difference of course between trance and trance control, in trance control the medium has less awareness and the Spirit world have nearly full control. This level is the level above physical mediumship.

In my opinion, the medium wishing to become a Trance medium should sit once a week for an hour and let the Spirit world get used to you, so they can perfect the blend that is needed. Rather than sitting for a particular discipline, healing or speaking, just sit for Spirit. The effort they need to make to perfect this discipline is considerable so sit and allow them to learn how best to blend with you. Remember trance is mental mediumship it is the co-operation of a mind blending with a mind. Never do the Spirit world enter your body or possess you. The old school of mediumship would tell us that we should never sit alone for trance, again I disagree with this. All we are saying with this statement is that there is something to fear, which I do not believe there is. In the old days of our pioneers they had very little knowledge on what was happening, they understood two powers, God and the Devil, or good and bad. So they sat in ignorance hoping they would connect to God or the good, to help them with this they invented lots of rituals to try to ease their fears. While I thank them for their dedication and being the stepping stones to what we have today, we have moved on considerably and we have much more knowledge on the Spirit world but also how the conscious mind and subconscious mind operates. I speak more about this in the chapter to do with protection.

So I would encourage the student to sit comfortably, ensure the doors are locked and phones switched off so you won't be disturbed. If you wish set up a voice recorder so if the Spirit world want to speak they have a device to speak into that you can listen back to. Focus on the breath and set yourself a time limit of one hour. Remember this will take time do not expect instant results.

Also keep a diary so you can record your progress, which may be very subtle. If you have a record of what is happening you can see your progress over time. Keep control of your reasoning mind. What you are learning is a perfectly natural extension of your mediumship. Let the Spirit world direct you into the discipline they feel you can be best used, whether that is healing or speaking or maybe a combination of both, but try not to limit you or the Spirit with your demands.


Other disciplines within Mental mediumship are; inspirational writing, spirit art (personally my favourite discipline and one I wish I could do) I have been privileged in the past to meet some of the greats in this field, Coral Polge, who is now within the Spirit world. Su Wood a fabulous Spirit Artists and a world renown tutor at the Arthur Findlay College and a name for the future Coral Ryder.

### Healing mediumship.

In my opinion, all mediumship is healing mediumship. But the actual practice of healing is very much an under estimated discipline. The times I have heard a tutor say to a student 'go away and become a healer' as though it is a second class ability, it does upset me. If we look back in history some of our best mediums started as healers. The practice of healing helps to build a platform of sensitivity and empathy that mediumship can be developed from, the healer learns how to be passive and let the Spirit world direct them. So they obtain a greater blend. I would encourage all trainees to look at healing it is a beautiful discipline and a much underrated one.

## Physical mediumship

Physical mediumship, like mental mediumship has a lot of disciplines within it. It is not mental mediumship. Basically, it means that whatever is seen or heard is done so externally and not perceived with in the mind, so everyone present should be able to witness the phenomena. It is known as first-hand mediumship because it is direct from the Spirit world to the people and does not require the mediums faculties. It is the most beautiful of all mediumship but it is extremely difficult to obtain and not all mediums will be able to become physical mediums.

It involves the production of a substance called ectoplasm which is produced from many different sources, the mediums own energy the sitters' energy and the materials within the room i.e. curtains, clothing etc.

The Spirit world then utilise this energy to produce a 'living substance' we have named ectoplasm the Spirit mind then inhabits this energy and it is moulded into the features of the spirit communicating. It is a truly beautiful phenomena to witness but once again the seeker must use their own discerning mind and ask themselves what they can see, and what they feel. The seeker must always approach all kinds of mediumship as a scientist that is what will help you to become better informed and less gullible.

There are many other disciplines that are too numerous to mention here, automatic writing, Transfiguration, materialisation, Spirit art. All of these disciplines, if you want to be good at them require you to undergo training and to become your own authority. Sit for Spirit and let them guide you to the discipline you are best suited for. Don't make demands, instead ask them "what do you want for me, how can I best serve you" you never know they may have something in store for you much greater than you can perceive for yourself

Your journey into any of these disciplines is a joyous one or should be. The chances are that on this journey you will lose confidence and hope, I can promise you that you will meet people who tell you that you are not good enough, smile at them because they are human and therefore flawed.

Don't allow their opinions to prevent you achieving what you want to achieve. Listen to the voice of the Spirit and ask them to guide you to where you should be. And never stop questioning that way you become your own authority and not a clone of someone else. Your most frequent used word throughout your training should be WHY, the more you ask why the more knowledge you will gain if you are ever told by a teacher to stop asking questions stop seeing that teacher and look for another one. No teacher can sustain all of your development and the teacher should both recognise this and encourage the student to move on.

Don't become a clone of someone else, the Spirit world have chosen you because you are good enough, so be brave enough to become you.

# Chapter 10.

## Guides and protection.

I can remember when I began my journey desperately wanting to know who my guides were, do I really have a wise person who watches over me? Someone like Red Cloud the guide of Estelle Roberts or Silver Birch the guide of Maurice Barbanell. For much of my early stages of mediumship this was probably my biggest distraction, who and what were my guides?

I can recall a time I attended a church service and the medium said to me, "You have a Native American brave as your guide but he only has one feather, please don't worry about this as you progress so will he and his feather will grow and stand erect within his head band".

Although grateful I had a guide, I wasted so much of my development looking for his feather and its growth which of course never happened.

Silver Birch gives to us in his books' teachings of Silver Birch', which are easily available and I would urge the student to read these wonderful books they explain very simply about Guides and identifying them.

One day an artist painted Silver Birch as a Native American Indian in the circle that night somebody asked Silver Birch the question, "Are you a Native American Indian?" Silver Birch replied in this way;

"if it pleases you to see me in this way then do so, in reality all that I am is a mind with no physical description, I am appointed to this medium for his growth and my own and above me are other minds who assist in my learning."

This is of course simplified but it shows that the Spirit guides put no store on the physical description but only on the knowledge. I often conjure up in my head an image of the new student saying "I want to know my guide" and doing all these exercises to find their identity and the Spirit guides saying to each other "ok lads who is going to dress up today?" but this is what I do think happens that we get the essence of a mind that we feel works with us then our brain invents a description as to what is acceptable to us. Whether that is a Native American, Egyptian or a Chinese man. I ask the student not to get hung up on this need that stems from the ego, but rather sit for the blend of the Spirit and ask them what you can learn from them today. What they have to teach you is far more valuable than how they look and when the time is right, if it is important to them and you they will bring to you voluntarily their identity rather than you forcing something because you need it.

One of the most disturbing things I have repeatedly heard throughout my development is that of evil spirits, trapped spirits and rescue circles. I want the reader to understand I only share with you my own truth and I am not the oracle so you need to discover what is true for you.

I believe in a Spirit world of love, truth and natural order. Because of this I refuse to make the Spirit world into Hollywood where ghost and evil exists. I once had this conversation with students, they asked the question is there a place for evil Spirits? I replied "of course people do not change because they are dead if they were evil here then they must be a place in Spirit where they can be that is separate from the good people".

When I got back to my room on the evening my guides asked me why I had said this, and this is their reply to me;

"No soul is born evil and no soul returns evil, evil or the perception of what you believe evil is, is of the physical not the Spirit, all that happens is the Soul returns home richer for the experience but with absolute no judgement on the situation".

It made sense to me but I found it difficult to truly understand, as humans we want our revenge and I was no different. I wanted revenge on all those who had hurt me in my childhood it is a normal human emotion, however if we really understand what my guides are saying here, it is our perception as to what evil is. What we consider evil is in fact a chance to learn and grow and enrich the soul. I therefore cannot believe in evil Spirits or trapped Spirits. In the 1970s it became big business to free trapped souls and cleanse the Aura of negative spirits or like with my ex-husband, free those that are trapped. We also have dedicated people who sit to rescue those who are trapped or lost, I believe that their motivation is good but I don't believe they are freeing lost souls.

If what I believe is true that the Spirit world is a place of order and natural intelligence, then I fail to see how the Spirit can become trapped, it would surely make a mockery of the concept of guides, those higher intelligence who are given the role of our development that they can allow the Spirits to become trapped like this or to make our lives a misery by 'haunting' us. Also to say that if the Spirit world is trapped here then the Guides need us to free them, once again the arrogance of saying we are more superior to the Spirit world and they cannot do it without us just doesn't make sense.

What about the cleansing of the Aura, this was a technique practiced in my church group every week, and every week we had to either free a 'stuck Spirit' or cleanse someone's negativity. So once again I ask you to approach this as scientists and leave the horror movies out of it for now.

The aura we know is an energy that surrounds every living thing, it is not solid and it is built on thought form, we know that all the information of our life are stored here and it is this same aura that good psychic will link to for information about our lives. But it is not solid, it has no substance, the Spirit world are also an energy, the body has died and been laid to rest, which leaves us with the Spirit.

The cleansing of the aura, to me is the cruellest thing to tell anyone. My aura holds within it the sum total of my life to date. It holds every occurrence and memory I have of my life, so when we are telling someone that their aura is black, dirty or full of negativity, in my opinion what they are doing is linking into a sad time in the sitters' life and misinterpreting this as negativity. I have been told by so many psychics that my aura is negative but they can never, when challenged, explain what they mean and this is why so many people who are vulnerable end up being ripped off. What I believe they are doing is linking to my childhood abuse and not knowing how to interpret this so coming out with fanciful notions of "you are negative" or "your energy is in need of a cleanse because it is full of blackness", well let me tell you all you can no sooner clean away my past than you can build a church on the moon and nor would I want you to, my past has made me who I am today it is my badge of honour.

But what you can do is clean up your thoughts, one of the fundamental truths of Spiritualism and mediumship is that our thoughts are living energy. So as we think we are.

We all at some point suffer from negative thoughts, but by being aware of them as they begin to form we can begin to change them to positive thoughts thus creating an aura of positivity that all that connect with us will sense whether they are psychic or not.

Remember YOU are the instrument, so it is YOUR responsibility, not Spirits to work on the instrument. Let us, begin with the power of the mind, the creator, the builder. Then we can start to offer the Spirit world a strong positive channel that they can deliver their messages through.

## Conclusion.

### The End, or is it?

I hope you enjoy your journey into your mediumship, as you are unique so is your journey.

I have shared with you my ideas and opinions I do not say they are the absolute truth. I say they are my truth as to where I am in my development right now. As I am developing, and I will be for the rest of my life it cannot be the ultimate truth.

What I would urge, is that you find your own truth, by sitting with the Sprit world and letting them guide you along your pathway, they are your teachers who will be with you till your road comes to its end. Mortal teachers cannot stay with you forever, for it is only right that you one day transcend the physical teacher and become your own authority. That is what we mean by progression.

Make the journey your journey, not just into mediumship and healing, but into understanding and accepting YOU. For you are unique and important and the Spirit world love you for that uniqueness.

So to sum up; be disciplined, have fun, and never let anyone tell you that you cannot, most of all don't tell yourself that.

This is a very lonely road to walk, surround yourself with supportive people and become a supportive person for someone else.

If you would like to know more about Jackie please visit her web site at;

www.jackiewrightdsnu.co.uk

Printed in Great Britain
by Amazon